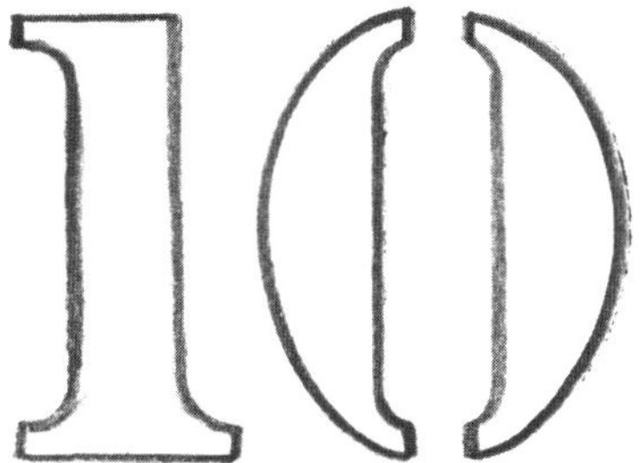

PAINTERS & SCULPTORS DRAW

Richard Diebenkorn

Jim Dine

Jasper Johns

Alex Katz

Ellsworth Kelly

Roy Lichtenstein

Claes Oldenburg

Robert Rauschenberg

James Rosenquist

Cy Twombly

Museum of Fine Arts
Boston

ISBN 0-87846-246-5
Typeset and printed by
Acme Printing Company, Medford, Massachusetts
Designed by Cynthia Rockwell Randall

Photo Credits:
Catalogue no. 3 courtesy of Smith College Museum of Art; nos. 8 and 24 courtesy of Museum of Fine Arts, Boston; no. 14 courtesy of Leo Castelli Gallery, New York; nos. 21, 49, and 53 by Geoffrey Clements; no. 34 by Robert McKeever; no. 41 courtesy of The Art Institute of Chicago; no. 43 by Bevan Davies.

Dates of exhibition: August 1 - September 30, 1984

Cover illustration: Jasper Johns, *0 through 9*, charcoal on paper, 1960.

The Exhibition

"10 Painters & Sculptors Draw" brings together ten American artists whose artistic careers began in the 1950s and in whose work drawing plays an important role.

The exhibition is the inaugural exhibition in the Museum's newly named Torf Gallery. The Torfs are major collectors of modern prints and it was considered fitting that their gallery open with an exhibition devoted to contemporary works on paper. All of the artists represented here are also included in the exhibition "The Modern Art of the Print: Selections from the Collection of Lois and Michael Torf," on view concurrently in the Gund Gallery.

It is hoped that this exhibition will afford an opportunity for rewarding comparisons and contrasts with regard to point of view and handling of media between ten draftsmen who started out in the era of Abstract Expressionism and whose work has either in some degree extended that style or strongly reacted against it. The selection of each artist's work has been handled individually, sometimes focusing on a particular period or motif (for example, early Diebenkorn figurative works or later Dine drawings from the model) or, in other cases, spanning most of the artist's career. The earliest work in the exhibition is dated 1958, the latest 1984. We trust that this selection will expand our audience's knowledge of the development of contemporary American art over the last twenty-five years and focus attention on the continuing vitality of contemporary drawing.

I would like to thank the participating artists and to acknowledge the generosity of the lenders, who responded enthusiastically in spite of a very short preparation time for the project. I am also grateful to certain individuals who were helpful with encouragement and advice in the early planning stages: Kathy Halbreich, Douglas Baxter, and Bill Goldston, as well as others who were unusually helpful during the organizational phase: Deborah Johnson, Mame Kennedy, Olivia Motch, and David Nolan. At the Museum of Fine Arts, I wish particularly to thank Drew Knowlton, David Becker, David Ross, Victoria Jennings, Lynn Herrmann, Cynthia Purvis, and Cynthia Randall. And, finally, I would like to thank Lois and Michael Torf whose gift was the inspiration for this exhibition.

Clifford S. Ackley
Department of Prints, Drawings, and Photographs

10 Painters & Sculptors

Richard Diebenkorn

Drawn contours have been an essential element of Richard Diebenkorn's painted works in all phases of his career. His earliest paintings were abstract, but in the late fifties, while resident in the San Francisco area, he turned to painterly figuration. Drawing from the model was one of the central issues for the Bay Area figurative artists Diebenkorn was associated with in the fifties and sixties, and it served as a foundation for Diebenkorn's painted figure pieces. In the late sixties he turned once again to abstraction. Diebenkorn's drawings from female models, as well as his still-life and landscape drawings of the late fifties and sixties, often anticipate in their structural and painterly concerns many of the formal qualities – rectilinear architecture and translucent veils of pigment – of the later painted and drawn *Ocean Park* abstractions.

Jim Dine

After a period of isolation from the New York scene during his residence in England in the late sixties, Jim Dine turned in the seventies to portrait and figure drawing from the model. Accompanying this return to a more traditional form of drawing was a new commitment to the expression of passionate feeling. Overt poetry or symbolism was welcomed, as seen in the voluptuous shell that his nude model Jessie holds in a series of drawings (nos. 10, 11). In many of these recent figure drawings the artist's aggressive attack on the sheet of paper itself – sanding, rubbing, gouging – calls to mind Dine's roots in Abstract Expressionism and that style's commitment to a vigorous physical dialogue with the picture surface.

Jasper Johns

Jasper Johns's drawings, like his paintings and sculptures, involve a dialogue between art and illusion. The most ordinary signs, symbols, or objects become the occasion for a sophisticated, often lyrical, puzzle for the eye. A table of numbers swims in and out of focus in a wash of dark, silvery graphite (no. 13); the eye attempts to extricate the numbers from zero to nine from the rhythmically gestural web of lines that they form (no. 14). The imagery and motifs of Johns's drawings parallel and often repeat those of his paintings and sculptures. *According to what* of 1969 (no. 15) is a free variation on a painting-construction of 1964. A Savarin coffee can holding the artist's brushes is both a reference to an earlier sculpture and a symbolic portrait of the artist (no. 16).

Alex Katz

The sitters for Alex Katz's portraits are generally family, friends, and figures from the New York world of the arts. His wife Ada is his most frequent model (nos. 18, 20, 22). His quiet portrait drawings made with hard pencils are often distillations of previously executed paintings. Although these drawings retain the angular vocabulary of form that characterizes the paintings, in the drawings the subtle grays of the graphite meld with the white of the paper, softening edges and contrasts. More bold and schematic are the full-size preparatory drawings in charcoal on butcher paper that Katz makes for transfer to canvas (no. 21).

Ellsworth Kelly

Since the 1950s Ellsworth Kelly has been producing alongside his hard-edged abstract paintings a series of economical linear drawings of plants and flowers. These pencil and ink drawings not only capture the character of individual plant forms but they are full of formal invention. As in many of Kelly's paintings and sculptures, negative spaces between forms play a critical role as positive design elements. These drawings signal the firm grounding of Kelly's abstract images in observed reality. Like the paintings and sculpture they also reveal the artist's obsession with the purity of essential forms.

Roy Lichtenstein

Most of Roy Lichtenstein's drawings are preparatory studies for works in other media: paintings, prints, and sculpture. Usually preceded by smaller and rougher sketches, a number of these sophisticated take-offs on various artistic styles are quite polished studies in colored pencil, with corrections often made by means of collage overlays (nos. 29, 31, 32, 33). Lichtenstein, in his crisp, hard-edged prints and sculpture frequently thinks in terms of skilled professional fabrication from a model rather than direct execution by the artist's own hand and has found cut-paper collage singularly appropriate for producing maquettes for works in these media. In his recent sculpture Lichtenstein has turned again to the ironic parodies of painterly brushwork that he first explored in his painting and prints in the sixties (no. 34). The preparatory designs for these sculptures are collages made from painted papers. The elements that compose such collages are sometimes drawn from a large stock of brushstroke fragments that the artist cuts out in advance. Lichtenstein also makes use of this repertoire of brushstroke fragments in composing his recent "brushstroke" paintings, taping them to the canvas and moving them about.

Claes Oldenburg

Many of sculptor Claes Oldenburg's drawings are deadpan, ironic studies for real or imaginary monuments in which everyday objects are enlarged to a colossal scale. These include both free gestural drawings and more carefully elaborated ones. The wit in Oldenburg's project drawings is sometimes the result of disparities between the humble subject of the drawing and the elevated manner in which it is executed: cigarette butts (Fagend Studies, no. 41) are delineated with the panache of a baroque sketch by Bernini, and a study for a colossal drum set along the Thames evokes the watercolors of Turner (no. 35). Another instance of the artist's playful mind is his use of cut-paper collage in the study for a monument involving a colossal pair of scissors (no. 37). A number of Oldenburg's highly finished drawings, intended for reproduction, place less emphasis on the touch of the artist's hand, perhaps anticipating an even more continuous tone and, consequently, a greater illusion of reality when reproduced (nos. 39, 40).

Robert Rauschenberg

Robert Rauschenberg's drawings are part of a twentieth-century collage tradition in which the most ordinary materials are magically transformed by the context in which the artist places them. In the 1950s Rauschenberg began making his characteristic transfer drawings in which a solvent such as lighter fluid and rubbing with a pencil result in the direct transfer of ghostly images of clippings from newspapers and magazines. The abstract gestural rhythm of the rubbing evokes the vocabulary of Abstract Expressionism, while the newspaper image itself is full of literal references to the real world, to the wallpaper of processed media imagery that surrounds us in our daily lives. In Rauschenberg's drawings of the fifties and sixties these pale fragments of mass media reality are often visually woven together by broad painterly passages of watercolor wash. In recent years Rauschenberg has continued his use of transfer images while working with collages of printed fabrics (no. 47). The interest in transparent layering visible in the earlier drawings continues in these later works.

James Rosenquist

Many of James Rosenquist's drawings are large-scale finished drawings with a long mural-like format. In these works, as in his paintings, the artist freely associates and interweaves disparate elements wrenched from their usual context in our society, reassembling them to fit his own personal vision of that society. Sometimes the disparity of these elements is heightened by the diversity of textures and the artist's varied means of applying the images to the surface. In *Cliff Hanger* (no. 48), for example, a photolithograph of a standard American house is combined with the imprint of an automobile tire and its tread, passages of crumpled paper, and an attached string. In other works, such as *Fahrenheit 1982°* (no. 49), the disparate elements dissolve into one another, executed in an illusionistic style that suggests commercial illustration. An image of heavy industry, a bucket of molten steel, is flanked by more "feminine" images: an aggressively thrusting cluster of lipsticks and a lacquered fingernail-pen that writes while the stars revolve in their circular tracks at night. The translucent plastic that Rosenquist, like Johns (no. 17), frequently uses for drawings gives a glow to the colored inks that suggests a color slide or photographic transparency.

Cy Twombly

Cy Twombly's art revolves around line: drawn, written, scribbled, doodled. His paintings are often essentially drawings on canvas and his works on paper frequently involve painted passages or drawing in wet paint. The background for his art is the automatic writing of the Surrealists, linear messages dictated by the uncensored unconscious. On first glance his drawings have the look of raw grafitti. Greater familiarity encourages one to characterize them rather as elegant, even hypersensitive. Twombly has resided in Rome since the 1950s and has a passionate interest in the cultures of the ancient Mediterranean. Many of his scrawled titles such as *The Triumph of Galatea* and *Naxos* – integral parts of the drawn composition – might well be grafitti on ancient Greek and Roman walls.

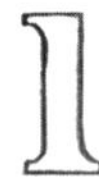

Richard Diebenkorn
Woman Leaning Her Chin on Her Hand, 1963
Conté crayon
16¾ x 13⅞ in.

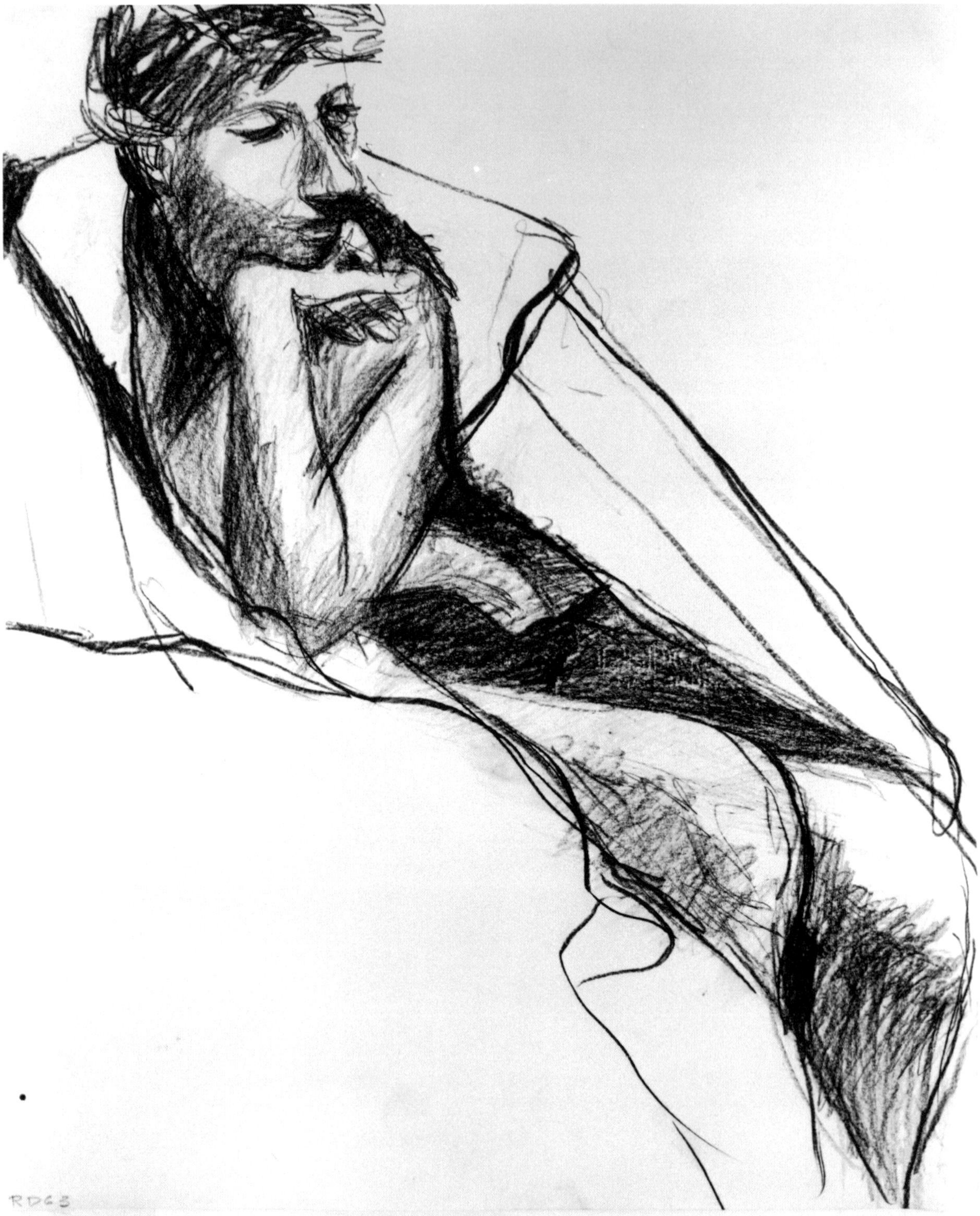

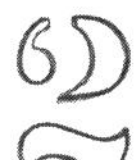

Jim Dine
The Early Sitter, 1975-76
Charcoal and pastel with sanding and scraping
40½ x 31 in.

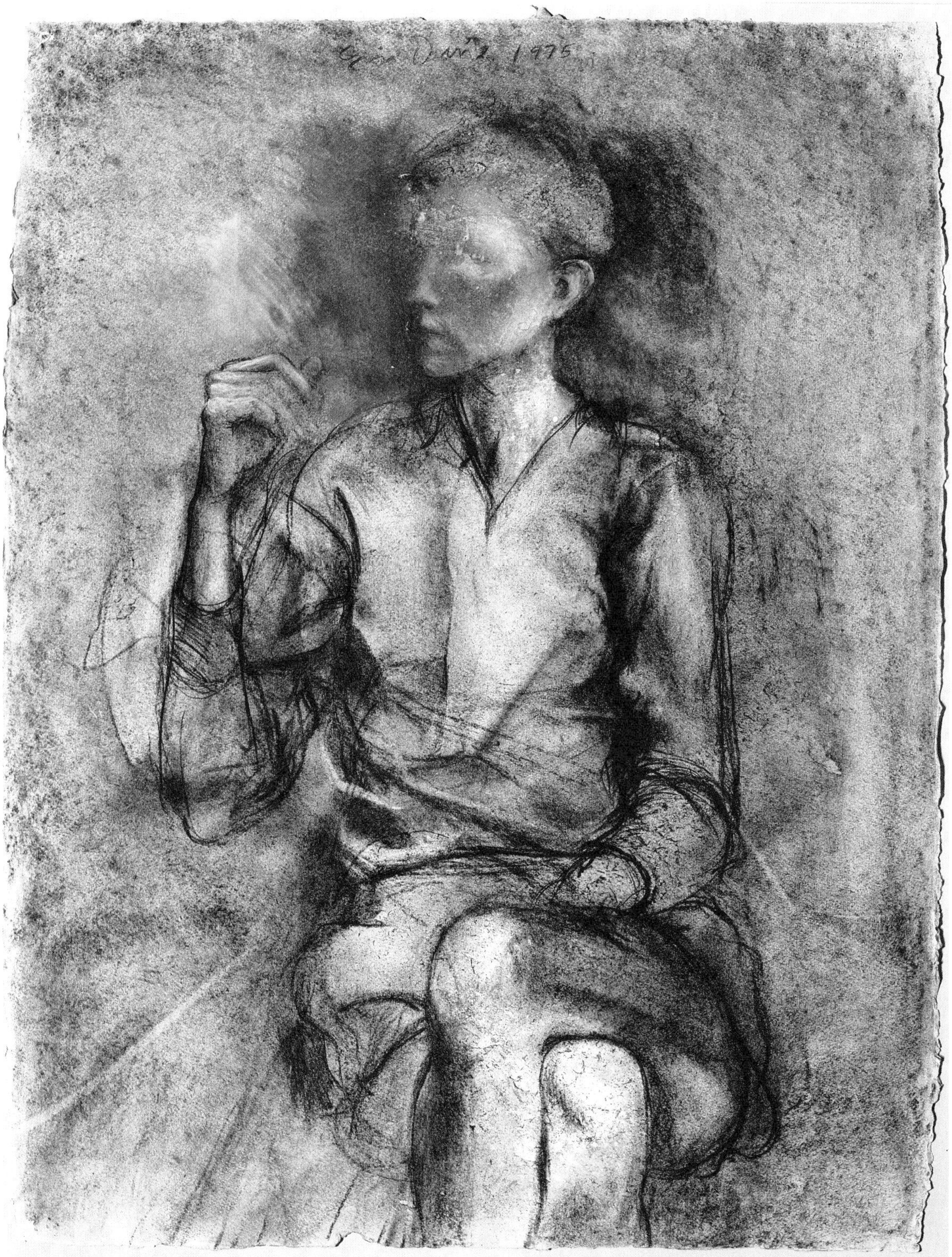

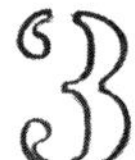

Jasper Johns
0 through 9, 1960
Charcoal
29 x 23 in.

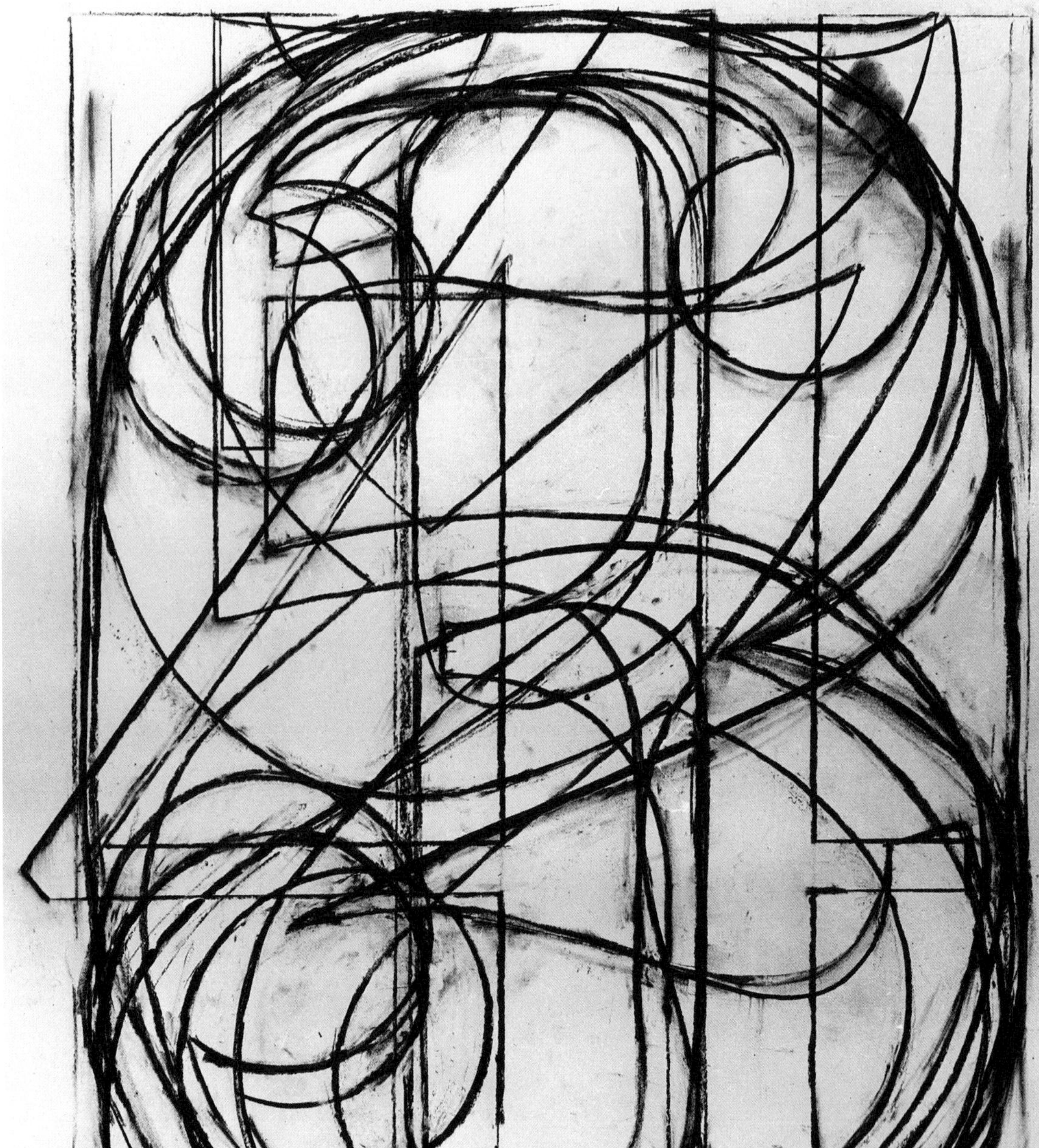

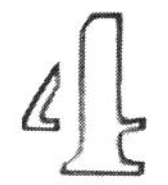

Alex Katz
Douglas, 1979
Charcoal and red chalk on kraft paper (contours pricked for transfer)
48½ x 34 in.

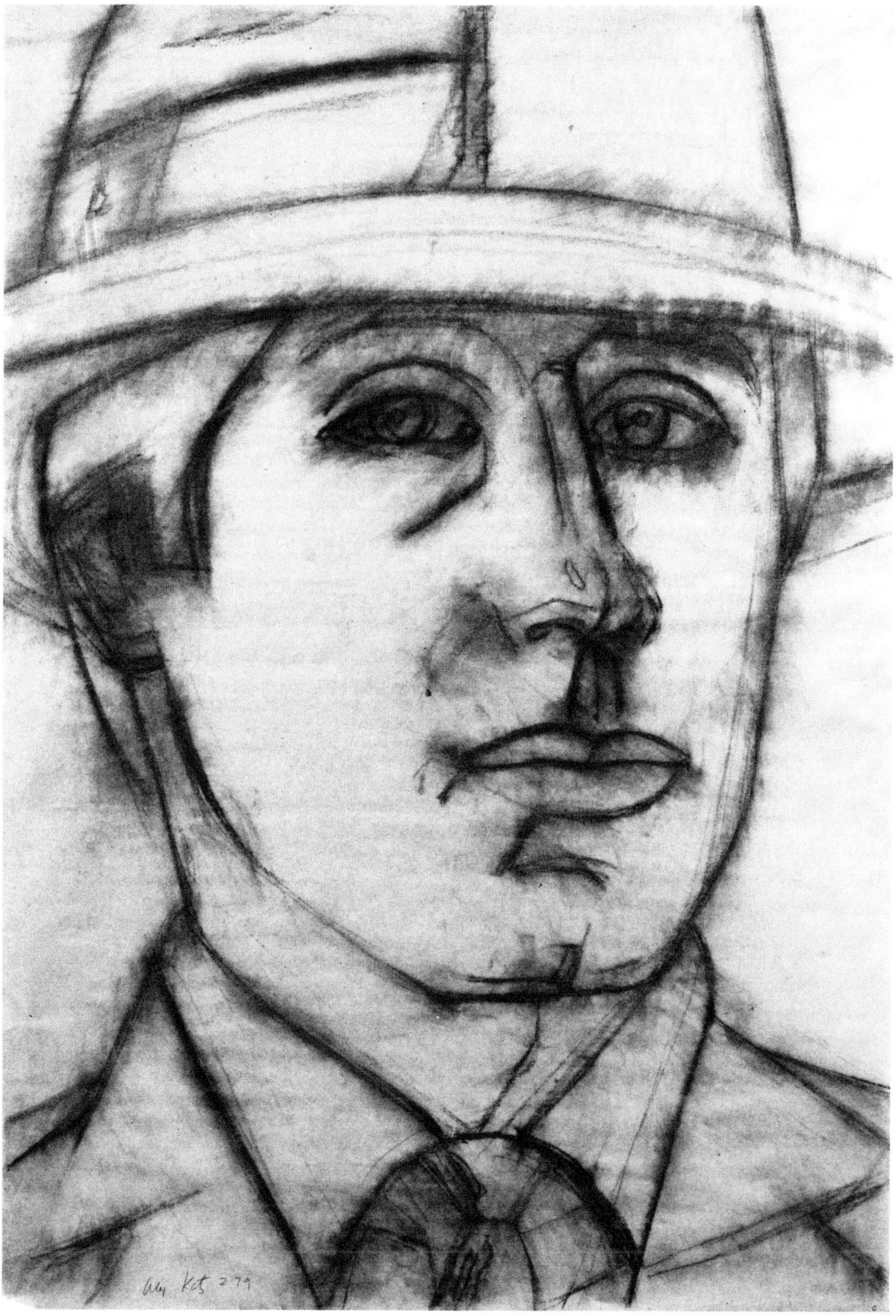

5

Ellsworth Kelly
Lemon Branch, 1964
Graphite
28½ x 22½ in.

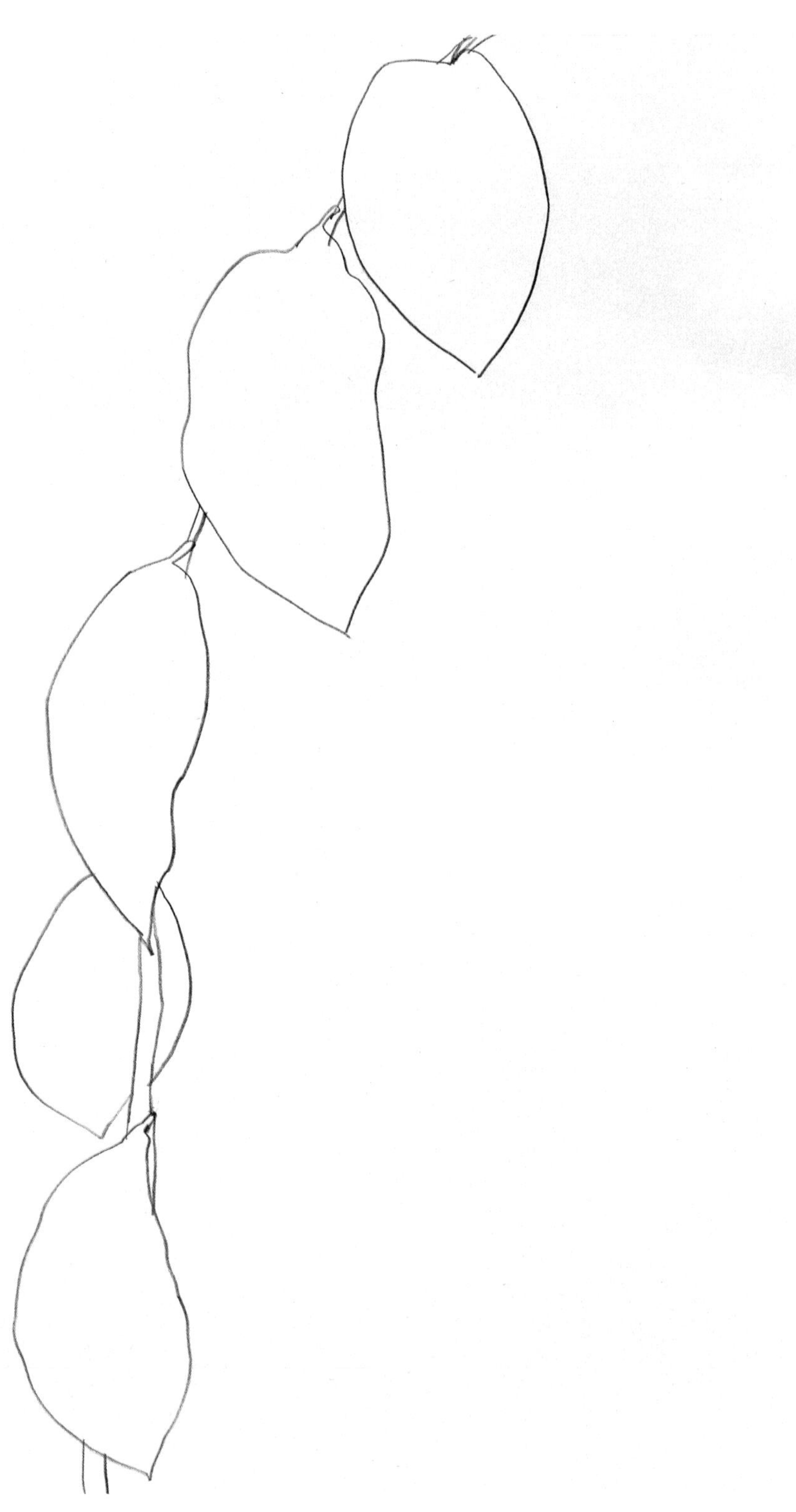

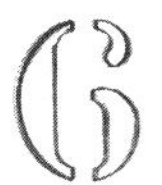

Roy Lichtenstein
Collage for *Brushstroke Sculpture*, 1982
Graphite, collage of painted papers and photographer's tape on foamcore
66½ x 32 in.

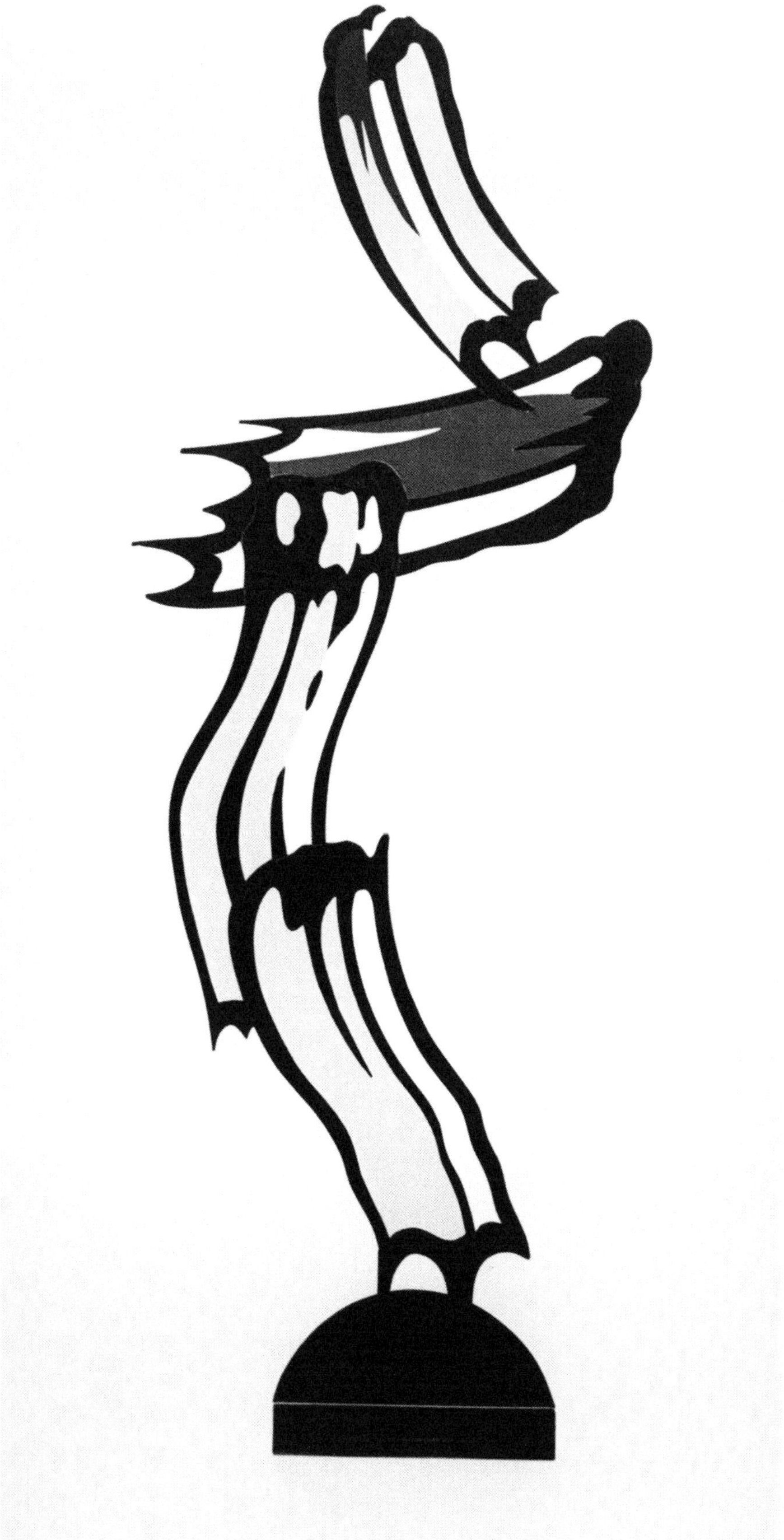

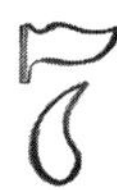

Claes Oldenburg
Fagend Studies, 1976
Charcoal and red and white chalks
39⅞ x 30 in.

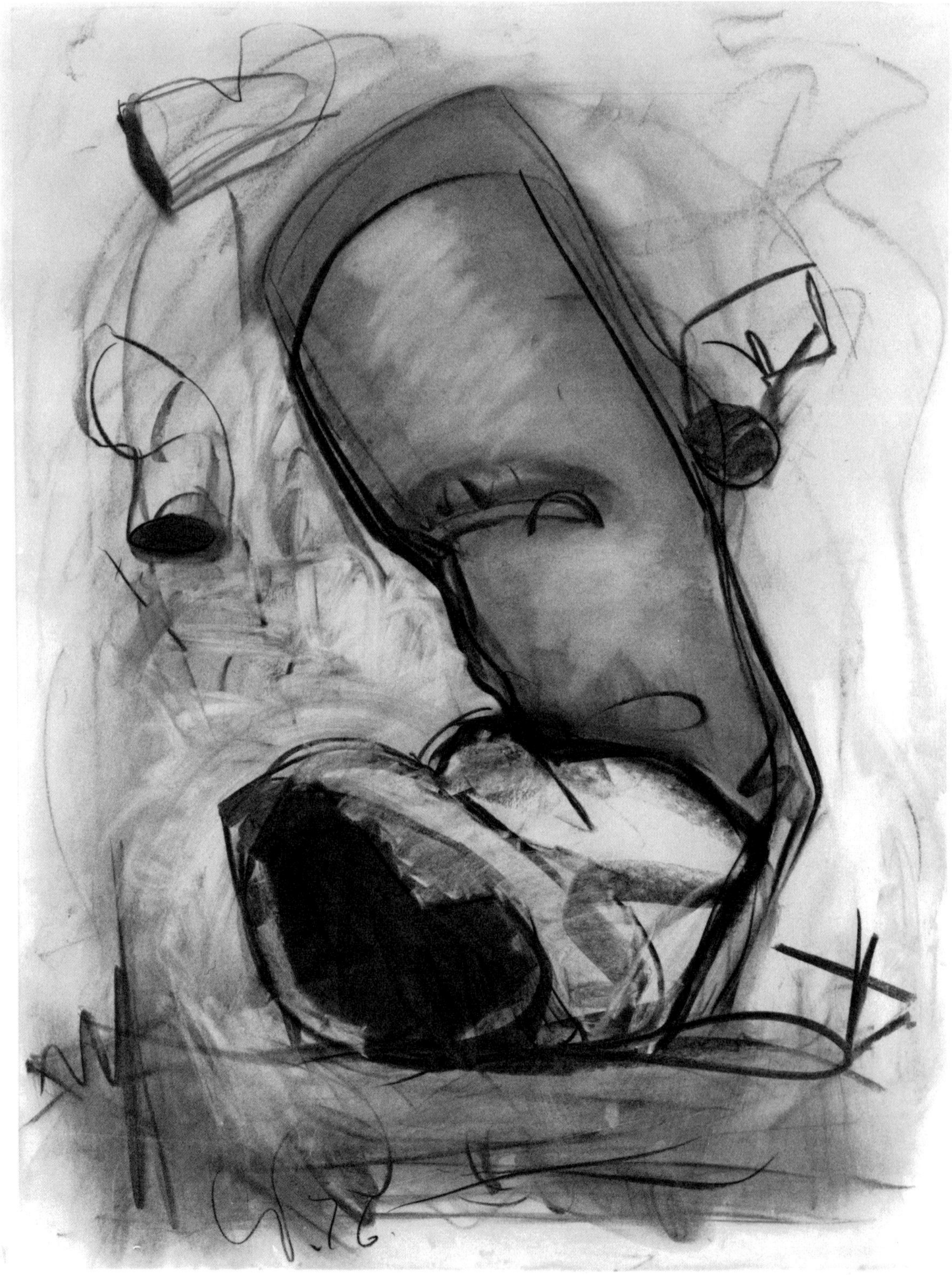

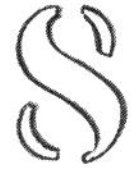

Robert Rauschenberg
Street Throng, 1959
Transfer drawing: rubbed transfers, graphite, watercolor, and gouache
24 x 36 in.

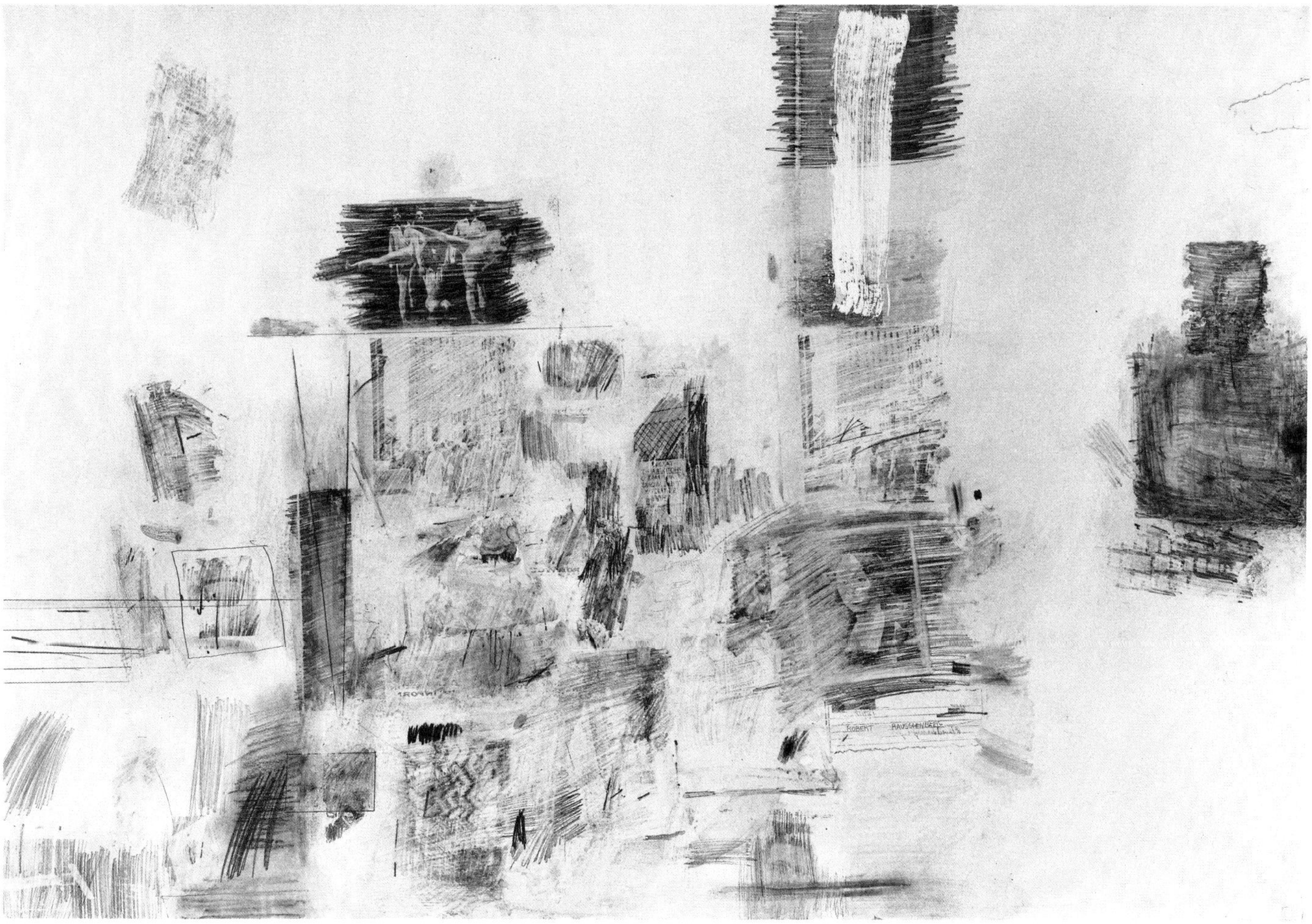

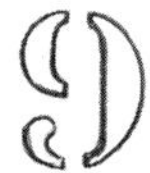

James Rosenquist
Fahrenheit 1982°, 1982
Colored inks on frosted Mylar
27$\frac{1}{8}$ x 64$\frac{1}{2}$ in. (image)

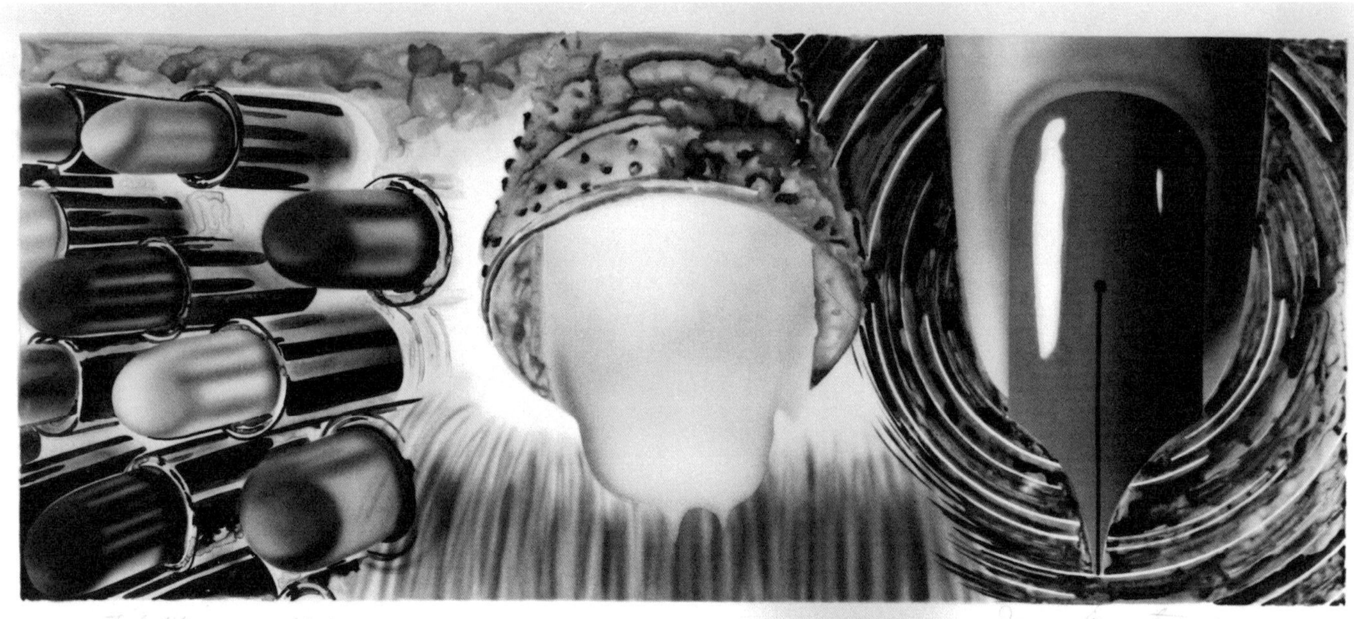

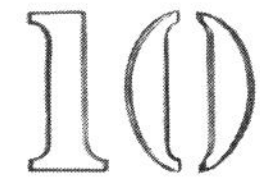

Cy Twombly
Untitled, 1964
Graphite, colored pencils, and crayon
27½ x 39⅜ in.

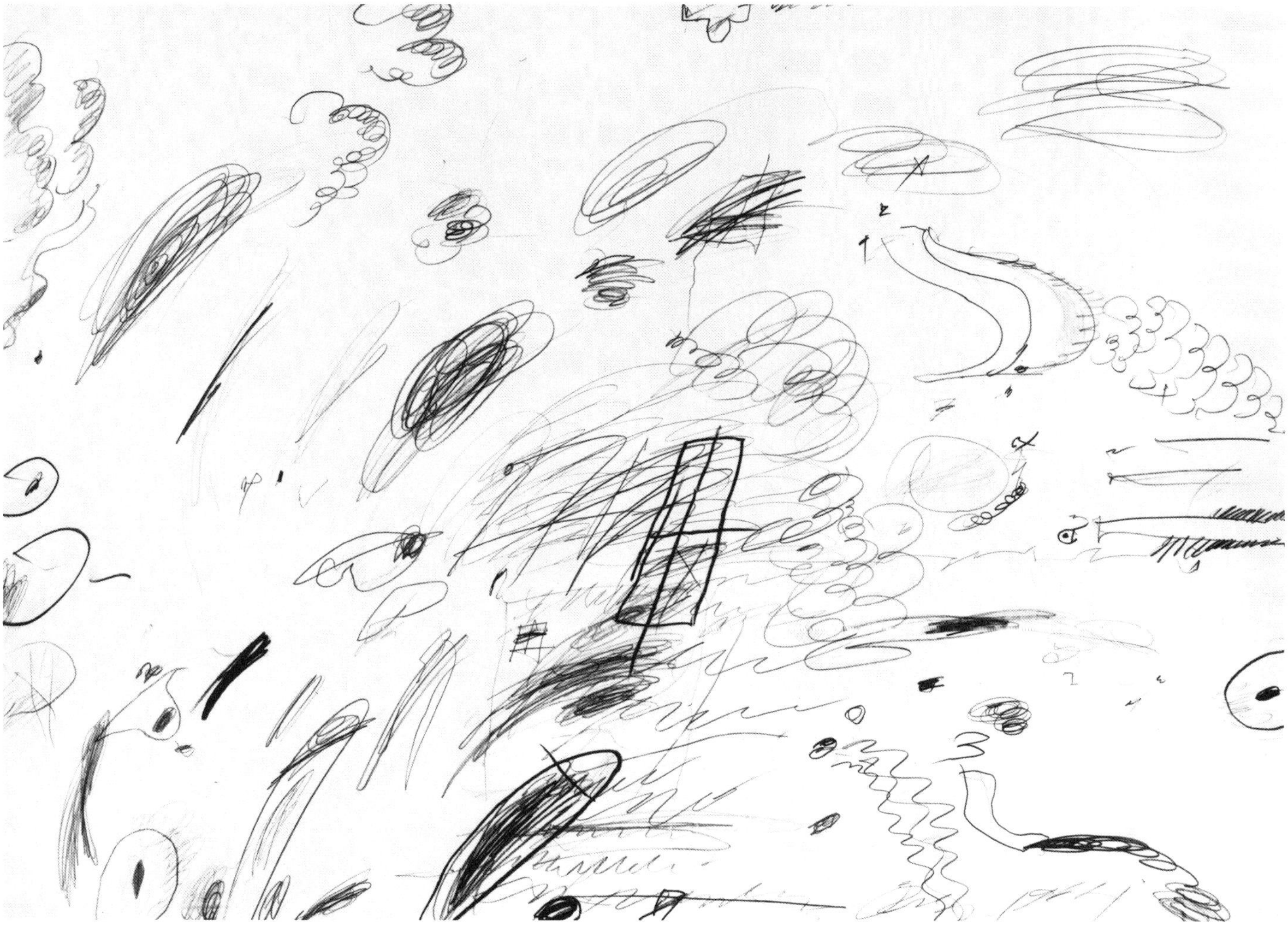

Checklist

Dimensions are sheet size unless otherwise noted. Height precedes width. Each artist's works are listed in chronological order.

Richard Diebenkorn (born 1922)

1.
Seated Nude, 1962
Conté crayon, graphite, and wash
17 x 13⅞ in.
Mr. and Mrs. Paul Wilson, San Francisco

2.
Landscape, 1963
Conté crayon and wash
12¾ x 17 in.
Mr. and Mrs. Dixon M. Farley

3.
Woman Leaning Her Chin on Her Hand, 1963
Conté crayon
16¾ x 13⅞ in.
Smith College Museum of Art, Gift of Mrs. Richard L. Selle (Carol Ann Osuhowski '54)

4.
Cup and Knife, 1964
Conté crayon, ink, and gouache
11 x 11 in.
Collection of the artist

5.
Seated Woman, 1965
Watercolor
14 x 16¾ in.
John Berggruen, San Francisco

6.
Woman in Chaise, 1965
Crayon and gouache
17 x 13¾ in.
Yale University Art Gallery
Lent by Richard Brown Baker, B.A. 1935

7.
Seated Nude, Leg Raised, 1968
Crayon
13¾ x 17 in.
Museum of Fine Arts, Boston
Sophie M. Friedman Fund 1975.667

Jim Dine (born 1935)

8.
The Early Sitter, 1975-76
Charcoal and pastel with sanding and scraping
40½ x 31 in.
Museum of Fine Arts, Boston
Gift of Michael Mazur 1982.787

9.
Jessie Bending at the Waist, 1978
Charcoal, pastel, airbrush, sanding, scraping
40 x 30 in.
The Pace Gallery, New York

10.
Jessie with Shell (Jer's), 1982
Charcoal, watercolor, and scraping
43 x 30½ in.
Jeremiah Dine

11.
Jessie with Shell (Nick's), 1982
Charcoal, acrylic washes, and scraping
43 x 30½ in.
Nicholas Dine

12.
The Key West Shell, 1981-84
Charcoal, pastel, acrylic, oil, and commercial enamel
47¾ x 46½ in.
Nancy Dine

Jasper Johns (born 1930)

13.
Black Numbers, 1960
Graphite wash on cream paper mounted on white paper
21¼ x 18¾ in (image)
Private collection, Boston

14.
0 through 9, 1960
Charcoal
29 x 23 in.
Collection of the artist

15.
According to What, 1969
Graphite
29¾ x 41¼ in.
Collection of the artist

16.
Savarin, 1977
Graphite, crayon, colored chalks on frosted Mylar
37 x 32¼ in. (sight)
Agnes Gund

17.
Usuyuki, 1981
Colored inks on plastic
49¼ x 18⅛ in.
Collection of the artist

Alex Katz (born 1927)

18.
Ada, December, 1972
Graphite
14¾ x 22¼ in.
Museum of Art, Rhode Island School of Design
Purchased with the aid of funds from the National Endowment for the Arts

19.
Edwin, 1973
Graphite
22¼ x 15 in.
Paul Jacques Schupf

20.
Ada in Polka Dot Blouse, 1975
Graphite
30 x 22 in.
Paul Jacques Schupf

21.
Douglas, 1979
Charcoal and red chalk on kraft paper (contours pricked for transfer)
48¼ x 34 in.
Private Collection

22.
Ada in Coat, 1982
Graphite
22½ x 15½ in.
Paul Jacques Schupf

Ellsworth Kelly (born 1923)

23.
Brier, 1959
Pen and black ink
22⅝ x 28½ in.
The Wadsworth Atheneum
Gift of Mr. Samuel Wagstaff

24.
Lemon Branch, 1964
Graphite
28½ x 22½ in.
Private Collection

25.
Brier, 1967
Graphite
30 x 22 in.
Private Collection

26.
Begonia, 1970
Pen and black ink
22 x 29⅞ in.
Private Collection

27.
Wild Grape, 1980
Graphite
30 x 40 in.
Private Collection

28.
Canna, 1982
Graphite
30 x 22¼ in.
Private Collection